purify my HEART

PARTICIPANT GUIDE

A Course for Youth on Bahá'í Laws, Chastity
and Sexuality from a Bahá'í Perspective

By Nava Ghalili-Wuorenma

Illustrations by: Yamani Anton and Dareleen Cano
(Youth of Badi School Panama)

And

Dr. Ava Ghalili

ACKNOWLEDGEMENTS

My eternal confidant Blake and loving son Solace Shoghi Ghalili-Wuorenma. It is your love that fuels this heart for service. Farah, Farshid and Ava Ghalili, I began creating this course at 13 years of age and I am indebted to your infinite encouragement, love and support, to which the completion of this course through my youth could not be realized without.

A sincere and heartfelt appreciation to André Segovia, Dr. Nura Mowzoon, Emily Sadeghian, Sautra Yazdanian Vahdat, Yamani Anton, Dareleen Cano and Badi School in Panama for your selfless service contributed to *Purify My Heart*. I am honored by your friendship, as I am your service and expertise.

Dedicated to the steadfast servant of the Covenant Aziz Ghalili,
who practiced moderation in all things, except in his service
and devotion to the Cause of God, his love for humanity
and especially teaching children, which had no limits or bounds.

"At the heart of the educational process
is contact with the Word of God,
whose power sustains every individual's
attempts to purify his or her heart."

~ Universal House of Justice. (2013)
Letter written to a National Spiritual Assembly, April 23.

Purify *My Heart* is a humble response to a community's interest in deepening on the importance of one's purity of motive, thought and action. It is a course that aims, through understanding the Bahá'í laws and principles, to empower and enrich the participants' insights into what it means to live a chaste and holy life. By participating in this course, there is a hope that deepening on certain themes will shape and build a capacity to better understand the power each participant has in spiritually transforming their own lives as well as the community in which they serve.

One does not need to look far to observe that a society involved in a process of disintegration may often weigh on the hearts and minds of individuals. *Purify My Heart* allows for the deepening and discussion of relevant Writings as a means to assist participants to understand the power of calling on one's higher spiritual nature to direct one's life while being aware of the demoralizing forces that can inhibit one's spiritual growth, within the context of chastity and its broader implications.

While matters about chastity and purity are often misconstrued and its significance diluted and altered by cultural forces, *Purify My Heart* addresses the topic by having participants engage in meaningful discussion on a selection of Writings that leave little room for misinterpretation and confusion. Readings of the Writings related to each lesson are then prompted by questions in the guide that the facilitator can pose to stimulate meaningful discussion. The questions stated in the facilitator guide should be used as a suitable and appropriate guide and should in no way inhibit the organic process of discussion that can take shape when a group is called upon to reflect on the Writings. The questions carefully formulated are those that have been tested and shown to yield positive results in study groups that have undergone this course. Participants who have engaged in the course have found the discussion and material stimulating, interesting and beneficial, especially when implemented. Some communities have noted, however subtle, a transformation in the conduct and spirit of their youth and their conduct.

The dynamic and standards of this study group are such that all participants (including the facilitator) should be considered as being engaged in a learning process where the rights and opinions of all should be respected in a spirit of unity. That is, the relationship between the facilitator and participant is not one of a teacher to a student. To learn about the dynamics of a study process that is participatory and raises the capacity of youth to take charge of their learning, one may wish to turn to the courses of the Ruhi Institute.

Experience with *Purify My Heart* has shown that the course is most beneficial when facilitated by a trusted older youth in the community who has experience in the institute process and is familiar with the role of a facilitator and the fruitful yet delicate dynamic of such a study group. It is highly recommended that older adults specifically parents not be present for the course as experience finds that youth are less comfortable in sharing experiences and less likely to engage in the frank discussions necessary to achieve the desired optimum level of understanding and insights into the implementation of the Writings. The high standard set by these scriptures is best internalized when facilitators find meaningful ways to encourage a spirit of prayerfulness and reverence before deepening on the Writings, for example: preparing devotional pieces, music, meditation or other spiritually reflective forms of the arts. It is suggested that facilitators begin the study session deepening in this way.

The Facilitator's guide outlines the lessons and points for discussion. Please allow sufficient time to review each lesson plan before beginning the study session. There is a purpose to the order of the themes and it is highly recommended that they be presented in this tested order. The following themes are explored in this course (as outlined in the course outline):

Section 1: Bahá'í Laws — Our spiritual purpose and how Bahá'í laws help us fulfill it

Section 2: Defining Chastity — Our spiritual and material identities

Section 3: Practicing Chastity — Application of spiritual laws

Section 4: Homosexuality — The Bahá'í perspective

Section 5: Chastity in All Religions — A timeless spiritual law

Section 6: Reflections — The power of youth and consultation

While it has taken over 20 years to compile and rigorously test the content of this program with a variety of communities around the globe, it is by no means exhaustive. It is a program that is continuously evolving and developing alongside the guidance of the Universal House of Justice and its improvement also heavily relies on the feedback of participants and facilitators. It is only one of several ways one can deepen on this vital topic but found to be effective.

While every effort is made to compile material, and employ approaches that consider the cultural and physical settings of a broad range of groups/ages, we are aware that there may be a need for flexibility in the way the course is facilitated to cater to such diverse groups in various parts of the globe. However, it is recommended that one follow the lesson plans as outlined, as it is one that has proven to be most effective.

While the course is designed for youth aged 15-21, we have found that some youth outside this age range also deem it to be quite useful. Experience also shows that the program is best run intensively and equally over the course of several consecutive days, however, this is only suggestion.

Most importantly, the *Purify My Heart* program is in no way intended to interfere with the vital core activities that should remain at the forefront of the efforts of community members. On the contrary, *Purify My Heart* was created in the spirit of enriching and enhancing the manner in which community members serve their society through such core activities. This course is an answer to a call from communities who have desired to deepen youth on Bahá'í laws associated with chastity. The intention is, that through meaningful conversations stimulated by the course, we can raise the standard of one's conduct by raising one's consciousness through increased understanding of the power of one's higher spiritual nature as a means to transform the life of the communities in which one serves. *Purify My Heart* aims to assist this noble intention.

Please contact the author and compiler of *Purify My Heart* to offer feedback or for clarification on any matter related to the content or structure of the course. Brochures and other material related to the course can also be obtained upon request.

info@purifymyheart.com
www.purifymyheart.com

Sincerely,
~ Nava Melody Ghalili-Wuorenma
(Author and Compiler)
www.navaghalili.com

COURSE OUTLINE

Section 1
Bahá'í Laws-
Our spiritual purpose and
how Bahá'í laws help us fulfill it

Section 2
Defining Chastity-
Our spiritual and material identities

Section 3
Practicing Chastity-
Application of spiritual laws

Section 4
Homosexuality-
The Bahá'í perspective

Section 5
Chastity In All Religious Texts-
A timeless spiritual law

Section 6
Reflections-
The power of youth and consultation

SECTION 1

Introduction to Bahá'í Law's

1. The purpose of God in creating man hath been, and will ever be, to enable him to know his Creator and to attain His Presence. To this most excellent aim, this supreme objective, all the heavenly Books and the divinely-revealed and weighty Scriptures unequivocally bear witness.

    Bahá'u'lláh (1990), *Gleanings From the Writings of Bahá'u'lláh*, Wilmette: Bahá'í Publishing Trust, p. 70.

FOOD FOR THOUGHT:

- To know God and draw nearer to Him, we are encouraged to deepen on the Writings of the Manifestations of God and follow Their laws.
    - What thoughts and feelings come to mind when someone says "Bahá'í laws"?
    - What thoughts and feelings come to mind when someone says "chastity"?
    - Why do we have such societal laws? i.e., What would happen if these laws were broken or did not exist?
    - What might we assume would happen when we break spiritual laws?
- In what way can we stay mindful that our thoughts and actions are aligned with achieving our life purpose (i.e., "know his Creator and attain His Presence")?
    - What keeps us from giving up our will and living according to God's Will and our life purpose?
- What are some thoughts or actions that contribute to knowing our Creator and attaining His Presence?
    - What are some thoughts or actions that do not contribute to knowing our Creator and attaining His Presence?

2. Consider the pettiness of men's minds. They ask for that which injureth them, and cast away the thing that profiteth them. They are, indeed, of those that are far astray. We find some men desiring liberty, and priding themselves therein. Such men are in the depths of ignorance.

    Liberty must, in the end, lead to sedition, whose flames none can quench. Thus warneth you He Who is the Reckoner, the All-Knowing. Know ye that the embodiment of liberty and its symbol is the animal. That which beseemeth man is submission unto such restraints as will protect him from his own ignorance, and guard him against the harm of the mischief-maker.

Bahá'u'lláh (1990), *Gleanings From the Writings of Bahá'u'lláh*, Wilmette, IL: Bahá'í Publishing Trust, p. 335-36.

3. "Know assuredly that My commandments are the lamps of My loving providence among My servants, and the keys of My mercy for My creatures."

Bahá'u'lláh (1978), *Proclamation of Bahá'u'lláh*, Wilmette: Bahá'í Publishing Trust, p. 122.

FOOD FOR THOUGHT:

- List some Bahá'í laws and ways in which they benefit us, using concrete examples.

4. "The drinking of wine" writes Abdu'l-Bahá, "is, according to the text of the Most Holy Book, forbidden; for it is the cause of chronic diseases, weakeneth the nerves, and consumeth the mind."

Shoghi Effendi (1963), *The Advent Of Divine Justice*, Wilmette, IL: Bahá'í Publishing Trust, p. 33.

5. As to opium, it is foul and accursed. God protect us from the punishment He inflicteth on the user. According to the explicit Text of the Most Holy Book, it is forbidden, and its use is utterly condemned. Reason showeth that smoking opium is a kind of insanity, and experience attesteth that the user is completely cut off from the human kingdom. May God protect all against the perpetration of an act so hideous as this, an act which layeth in ruins the very foundation of what it is to be human, and which causeth the user to be dispossessed for ever and ever.

For opium fasteneth on the soul so that the user's conscience dieth, his mind is blotted away, his perceptions are eroded. It turneth the living into the dead. It quencheth the natural heat. No greater harm can be conceived than that which opium inflicteth. Fortunate are they who never even speak the name of it; then think how wretched is the user.

'Abdu'l-Bahá (1982), *Selections From the Writings of 'Abdu'l-Bahá*, Haifa: Bahá'í World Centre, p. 146.

FOOD FOR THOUGHT:

- Can we apply the principles of physical laws of science to spiritual laws?
    - For example, the law of physics related to "Cause and Effect." i.e., Newton's third law of motion states that for every action there is an equal and opposite reaction. Can we in any way use this principle in understanding the cause and effects of practicing spiritual laws?
- When societal laws are broken, it may be possible to witness the physical consequences. However, when spiritual laws are broken, the consequences may not always be noticeable (ask the group to provide some concrete examples).
- Discuss: Bahá'u'lláh says, "The reward of no good deed, is or ever will be lost."

Bahá'u'lláh (1986), *A Compilation on Women, Compiled by the Research Department of the Universal House of Justice*, Haifa: Bahá'í World Centre, p.45.

6. As to chastity, this is one of the most challenging concepts to get across in this very permissive age, but Bahá'ís must make the utmost effort to uphold Bahá'í standards, no matter how difficult they may seem at first. Such efforts will be made easier if the youth will understand that the laws and standards of the Faith are meant to free them from untold spiritual and moral difficulties in the same way that a proper appreciation of the laws of nature enables one to live in harmony with the forces of the planet.

The Universal House of Justice. (1985) *Letter to Individual Believer*, January 14

7. As to a chaste and holy life, it should be regarded as no less essential a factor that must contribute its proper share to the strengthening and vitalization of the Bahá'í community, upon which must in turn depend the success of any Bahá'í plan or enterprise… All of them, be they men or women, must, at this threatening hour when the lights of religion are fading out, and its restraints are one by one being abolished, pause to examine themselves, scrutinize their conduct, and with characteristic resolution arise to purge the life of their community of every trace of moral laxity

that might stain the name, or impair the integrity, of so holy and precious a Faith.

Shoghi Effendi (1963), The Advent Of Divine Justice, Wilmette, IL: Bahá'í Publishing Trust, p. 29.

FOOD FOR THOUGHT:

- What does it mean and look like to pause to examine oneself, scrutinize our conduct, and with characteristic resolution arise to purge the life of our community? Provide examples.

  Optional: (If it is helpful, you may wish to use a few minutes to creatively express these examples through drawing, writing a poem or any other form of arts).

- What are the effects of practicing the laws of God, on the greater good of society and its well-being?

8. If ever it could be said that a religion belonged to the youth, then surely the Bahá'í Faith today is that religion. The whole world is suffering; it is sunk in misery, crushed beneath its heavy problems. The task of healing its ills and building up its future devolves mainly upon the youth. They are the generation who, after the war, will have to solve the terrible difficulties created by the war and all that brought it about. And they will not be able to build up the future except by the laws and principles laid down by Bahá'u'lláh. So their task is very great and their responsibility very grave.

Shoghi Effendi. (1942) *Letter to Bahá'í children and youth of Peoria*, May 8

WORKSHEET 1

(Bahá'í Laws)

1. What is our spiritual purpose?

2. Why do we have spiritual laws and how should we view them?

3. What would happen when one follows the laws of God?

4. What would happen when one disobeys the laws of God?

SECTION 2

Chastity

1. In man there are two natures; his spiritual or higher nature and his material or lower nature. In one he approaches God, in the other he lives for the world alone. Signs of both these natures are to be found in men. In his material aspect he expresses untruth, cruelty and injustice; all these are the outcome of his lower nature. The attributes of his Divine nature are shown forth in love, mercy, kindness, truth and justice, one and all being expressions of his higher nature. Every good habit, every noble quality belongs to man's spiritual nature, whereas all his imperfections and sinful actions are born of his material nature. If a man's Divine nature dominates his human nature, we have a saint.

    Man has the power both to do good and to do evil; if his power for good predominates and his inclinations to do wrong are conquered, then man in truth may be called a saint. But if, on the contrary, he rejects the things of God and allows his evil passions to conquer him, then he is no better than a mere animal.

    'Abdu'l-Bahá (2006), Paris Talks: Addresses Given by 'Abdu'l-Bahá in 1911, Wilmette, IL: Bahá'í Publishing Trust, p.67.

2. 'Abdu'l-Bahá explains that the human being has two natures, the spiritual or higher nature and the material or lower nature, and that the purpose of life is to gain mastery over the limitations and promptings of one's material nature and to cultivate spiritual qualities and virtues—the attributes of the soul which constitute one's true and abiding identity. Worldly desire is not the essence of a human being, but a veil that obscures it. Adherence to the Teachings of the Divine Educator refines the character and develops the potentialities with which each person is endowed; it liberates the individual and society from lower inclinations that give rise to the ills that afflict humanity.

    The Universal House of Justice. (2014) *Letter to Individual Believer*, May 9.

FOOD FOR THOUGHT:

- What are some thoughts or actions that are driven by our higher nature (spiritual)?
- What are some thoughts or actions that are driven by our lower nature (material/ego)?
- Why would a human be drawn to acting like an "animal" as opposed to a "saint" as Abdu'l-Bahá describes in the quote?
    - Why is it difficult to exercise our higher nature versus our lower nature?
- Which nature do we exercise, when we practice the Bahá'í laws?

3. Such a chaste and holy life, with its implications of modesty, purity, temperance, decency, and clean-mindedness, involves no less than the exercise of moderation in all that pertains to dress, language, amusements, and all artistic and literary avocations. It demands daily vigilance in the control of one's carnal desires and corrupt inclinations. It calls for the abandonment of a frivolous conduct, with its excessive attachment to trivial and often misdirected pleasures. It requires total abstinence from all alcoholic drinks, from opium, and from similar habit-forming drugs. It condemns the prostitution of art and of literature, the practices of nudism and of companionate marriage, infidelity in marital relationships, and all manner of promiscuity, of easy familiarity, and of sexual vices. It can tolerate no compromise with the theories, the standards, the habits, and the excesses of a decadent age. Nay rather it seeks to demonstrate, through the dynamic force of its example, the pernicious character of such theories, the falsity of such standards, the hollowness of such claims, the perversity of such habits, and the sacrilegious character of such excesses.

The maintenance of such a high standard of moral conduct is not to be associated or confused with any form of asceticism, or of excessive and bigoted puritanism. The standard inculcated by Bahá'u'lláh seeks, under no circumstances, to deny anyone the legitimate right and privilege to derive the fullest advantage and benefit from the manifold joys, beauties, and pleasures with which the world has been so plentifully enriched by an All-Loving Creator.

Shoghi Effendi (1963), *The Advent Of Divine Justice*, Wilmette, IL: Bahá'í Publishing Trust, p. 30.

- Define "chastity".
- What are some examples in this passage that relate to our lower (material) nature?
- What are some examples in this passage that refer to our higher (spiritual) nature?
- How is practicing chastity the practice of discipline over our material appetites?
- *Broader implications of chastity*: What are some other higher and lower appetites, outside pre-marital sex, alcohol and drugs?
  For example:
    - How we treat our bodies?
    - How we speak to people?
    - How we interact with others?
    - The overall image we convey by how we act and dress?
- What are some of the consequences of not practicing chastity?
    - What are some of the benefits of practicing chastity?

4. We have considered your several letters and have noted your questions, and your view that many Bahá'í youth in ... are confused, and are pleading for guidance in simple clear language on how to meet daily situations, particularly those involving sex. It is neither possible nor desirable for the Universal House of Justice to set forth a set of rules covering every situation. Rather is it the task of the individual believer to determine, according to his own prayerful understanding of the Writings, precisely what his course of conduct should be in relation to situations which he encounters in his daily life. If he is to fulfil his true mission in life as a follower of the Blessed Perfection, he will pattern his life according to the Teachings. The believer cannot attain this objective merely by living according to a set of rigid regulations. When his life is oriented toward service to Bahá'u'lláh, and when every conscious act is performed within this frame of reference, he will not fail to achieve the true purpose of his life.

Therefore, every believer must continually study the sacred Writings and the instructions of the beloved Guardian, striving always to attain a new and better understanding of their import to him and to his society. He should pray fervently for Divine Guidance, wisdom and strength to do what is pleasing to God, and to serve Him at all times and to the best of his ability.

The Universal House of Justice. (1968) *Letter to Individual Believer*, October 17.

Food for Thought:

- What is the guidance given by The Universal House of Justice?
- Give examples where you may be faced with a decision that pertains to chastity. How can you ask yourself whether the action is driven by the lower or higher nature, i.e., right or wrong?

5. Self has really two meanings, or is used in two senses, in the Bahá'í Writings; one is self, the identity of the individual created by God. This is the self mentioned in such passages as "he hath known God who hath known himself", etc. The other self is the ego, the dark, animalistic heritage each one of us has, the lower nature that can develop into a monster of selfishness, brutality, lust and so on.

Shoghi Effendi. (1947) *Letter to Individual Believer* in Canada, December 10.

Food for Thought:

- What are some of the reasons a youth would wish to have a boyfriend or girlfriend?
    - Which reasons stem from our lower nature and which from our higher nature?
    - Which reasons would help fulfill our spiritual purpose in life?
- If one's motives behind having a boyfriend or girlfriend stem from the lower nature, what could be some of the physical, emotional and spiritual consequences?

6. It is the challenging task of the Bahá'ís to obey the law of God in their own lives, and gradually to win the rest of mankind to its acceptance.

In considering the effect of obedience to the laws on individual lives, one must remember that the purpose of this life is to prepare the soul for the next. Here one must learn to control and direct one's animal impulses, not to be a slave to them. Life in this world is a succession of tests and achievements, of falling short and of making new spiritual advances. Sometimes the course may seem very hard, but one can witness, again and again, that the soul who steadfastly obeys the law of Bahá'u'lláh, however hard it may seem, grows spiritually, while the one who compromises with the law for the sake of his own apparent happiness is seen to have been following a chimera: he does not attain the happiness he sought, he retards his spiritual advance and often brings new problems upon himself.

The Universal House of Justice. (1973) *Letter to Individual Believer*, February 6.

7. … the beloved Guardian is describing the requirements not only of chastity, but of "a chaste and holy life" — both the adjectives are important. One of the signs of a decadent society, a sign which is very evident in the world today, is an almost frenetic devotion to pleasure and diversion, an insatiable thirst for amusement, a fanatical devotion to games and sport, a reluctance to treat any matter seriously, and a scornful, derisory attitude towards virtue and solid worth. Abandonment of "a frivolous conduct" does not imply that a Bahá'í must be sour-faced or perpetually solemn. Humour, happiness, joy are characteristics of a true Bahá'í life. Frivolity palls and eventually leads to boredom and emptiness, but true happiness and joy and humor that are parts of a balanced life that includes serious thought, compassion and humble servitude to God are characteristics that enrich life and add to its radiance.

Shoghi Effendi's choice of words was always significant, and each one is important in understanding his guidance. In this particular passage, he does not forbid `trivial' pleasures, but he does warn against `excessive attachment' to them and indicates that they can often be "misdirected. One is reminded of 'Abdu'l-'Abdu'l-Bahá's caution that we should not let a pastime become a waste of time."

The Universal House of Justice. (1979) *Letter to Individual Believer*, May 8.

FOOD FOR THOUGHT:

 In which circumstance is sex purely a material/physical appetite and which circumstances is it a spiritual act? Why?

8. Briefly stated the Bahá'í conception of sex is based on the belief that chastity should be strictly practiced by both sexes, not only because it is in itself highly commendable ethically, but also due to its being the only way to a happy and successful marital life. Sex relationships of any form, outside marriage, are not permissible therefore,

and whoso violates this rule will not only be responsible to God, but will incur the necessary punishment from society.

The Bahá'í Faith recognizes the value of the sex impulse, but condemns its illegitimate and improper expressions such as free love, companionate marriage and others, all of which it considers positively harmful to man and to the society in which he lives. The proper use of the sex instinct is the natural right of every individual, and it is precisely for this purpose that the institution of marriage has been established. The Bahá'ís do not believe in the suppression of the sex impulse but in its regulation and control.

Shoghi Effendi. (1938) *Letter to Individual Believer*, September 5.

9. Concerning your question whether there are any legitimate forms of expression of the sex instinct outside of marriage; according to the Bahá'í Teachings no sexual act can be considered lawful unless performed between lawfully married persons. Outside of marital life there can be no lawful or healthy use of the sex impulse. The Bahá'í youth should, on the one hand, be taught the lesson of self-control which, when exercised, undoubtedly has a salutary effect on the development of character and of personality in general, and on the other should be advised, nay even encouraged, to contract marriage while still young and in full possession of their physical vigour. Economic factors, no doubt, are often a serious hindrance to early marriage but in most cases are only an excuse, and as such should not be overstressed.

Shoghi Effendi. (1940) *Letter to Individual Believer*, December 13.

FOOD FOR THOUGHT:

- How does practicing the laws of chastity, secure the sacred bond of a future or current marriage?
- How does being unchaste in our thoughts, words and treatment of our souls and bodies affect our relationship with someone whom we are trying to be acquainted with? How can it affect our choice in marital partner?
- Is it possible to reduce the spiritual and physical act of sex within a marriage to that of purely a material/physical one?

ɢ	How does being unchaste in our thoughts, words and treatment of our souls and bodies affect our relationship with our current or future spouse?

ɢ	How can one avoid this with a newly gained understanding the concept of the lower and higher nature?

10.	The Bahá'í standard is very high, more particularly when compared with the thoroughly rotten morals of the present world. But this standard of ours will produce healthier, happier, nobler people, and induce stabler marriages.

Shoghi Effendi. (1947) *Letter to Individual Believer*, October 19.

Having now completed the first two important sessions of *Purify My Heart*, take a few moments now to reflect on your learning thus far. You may wish to either journal or walk and share your learning with a partner.

FOOD FOR THOUGHT:

Personal reflection questions (can also be completed at home):

☩	Do section 2 questions

WORKSHEET 2

(What is Chastity?)

1. What does chastity mean to you?

2. List some material-driven appetites (lower nature) as well as spiritual-driven intentions (higher nature) within the context of chastity.

3. How does practicing chastity foster happier and stable marriages?

SECTION 3

Practicing Chastity

1. He is My true follower who, if he come to a valley of pure gold, will pass straight through it aloof as a cloud, and will neither turn back, nor pause. Such a man is, assuredly, of Me. From his garment the Concourse on high can inhale the fragrance of sanctity…. And if he met the fairest and most comely of women, he would not feel his heart seduced by the least shadow of desire for her beauty. Such an one, indeed, is the creation of spotless chastity. Thus instructeth you the Pen of the Ancient of Days, as bidden by your Lord, the Almighty, the All-Bountiful.

    Bahá'u'lláh (1990), *Gleanings From the Writings of Bahá'u'lláh*, Wilmette: Bahá'í Publishing Trust, p. 118

2. What Bahá'u'lláh means by chastity certainly does not include the kissing that goes on in modern society. It is detrimental to the morals of young people, and often leads them to go too far, or arouses appetites which they cannot perhaps at the time satisfy legitimately through marriage, and the suppression of which is a strain on them.

    Shoghi Effendi. (1947) *Letter to Individual Believer*, October 19.

3. Ye are forbidden to commit adultery, sodomy and lechery. Avoid them, O concourse of the faithful. By the righteousness of God! Ye have been called into being to purge the world from the defilement of evil passions. This is what the Lord of all mankind hath enjoined upon you, could ye but perceive it. He who relateth himself to the All-Merciful and committeth satanic deeds, verily he is not of Me. Unto this beareth witness every atom, pebble, tree and fruit, and beyond them this ever-proclaiming, truthful and trustworthy Tongue.

    Bahá'u'lláh. *The Compilation of Compilations*, vol. 1, p. 57

4. Masturbation is clearly not a proper use of the sex instinct, as this is understood in the Faith. Moreover it involves, as you have pointed out, mental fantasies, while Bahá'u'lláh, in the Kitáb-i-Aqdas, has exhorted us not to indulge our passions and in one of His well-known Tablets 'Abdu'l-Bahá encourages us to keep our 'secret thoughts pure'. Of course many wayward thoughts come involuntarily to the mind and these are merely

a result of weakness and are not blameworthy unless they become fixed or even worse, are expressed in improper acts.

The Universal House of Justice. (1981) *Letter to Individual Believer*, March 8.

5.   Chastity implies both before and after marriage an unsullied, chaste sex life. Before marriage absolutely chaste, after marriage absolutely faithful to one's chosen companion. Faithful in all sexual acts, faithful in word and in deed.

The world today is submerged, amongst other things, in an over-exaggeration of the importance of physical love, and a dearth of spiritual values. In as far as possible the believers should try to realize this and rise above the level of their fellow-men who are, typical of all decadent periods in history, placing so much over-emphasis on the purely physical side of mating. Outside of their normal, legitimate married life they should seek to establish bonds of comradeship and love which are eternal and founded on the spiritual life of man, not on his physical life. This is one of the many fields in which it is incumbent on the Bahá'ís to set the example and lead the way to a true human standard of life, when the soul of man is exalted and his body but the tool for his enlightened spirit. Needless to say this does not preclude the living of a perfectly normal sex life in its legitimate channel of marriage.

Shoghi Effendi. (1941) *Letter to Individual Believer*, September 28.

6.   A chaste and holy life must be made the controlling principle in the behavior and conduct of all Bahá'ís, both in their social relations with the members of their own community, and in their contact with the world at large. It must adorn and reinforce the ceaseless labors and meritorious exertions of those whose enviable position is to propagate the Message, and to administer the affairs, of the Faith of Bahá'u'lláh. It must be upheld, in all its integrity and implications, in every phase of the life of those who fill the ranks of that Faith, whether in their homes, their travels, their clubs, their societies, their entertainments, their schools, and their universities. It must be accorded special consideration in the conduct of the social activities of every Bahá'í summer school and any other occasions on which Bahá'í community life is organized and fostered. It must be closely and continually identified with the mission of the Bahá'í youth, both as an element in the life of the Bahá'í community, and as a factor in the future progress and orientation of the youth of their own country.

Shoghi Effendi (1963), *The Advent Of Divine Justice*, Wilmette, IL: Bahá'í Publishing Trust, p. 29-30.

FOOD FOR THOUGHT:

- By using concrete examples and the concept of the lower and higher nature, how can we practice chastity?
    - In our thoughts?
    - In our choice of words and language?
    - In the way we dress?
    - In our relationships with others?
    - In a courtship with someone whom we are becoming acquainted with?
    - In a marriage?
- Based on the passages you have read, as well as your understanding of the lower and higher nature, how might one view pornography?
- Now having explored ways in which one can practice chastity in the above listed examples, take a few minutes to use the arts to illustrate your understanding of one of the points (for example you may like to draw, write a poem, or even create a short skit). When you are done you may wish to present your artistic expression to the group.

WORKSHEET 3

(Practicing Chastity?)

1. In what ways can one practice chastity?

2. Explain how we can use the concept of the lower and higher nature when making everyday decisions that involve chastity. Provide an example.

3. List some potential dangers that result from not practicing chastity in relationships.

SECTION 4

Homosexuality

1.   While Bahá'ís hold specific beliefs about human identity, sexuality, personal morality, and individual and social transformation, they also believe that individuals must be free to investigate truth and should not be coerced. They are, therefore, enjoined to be tolerant of those whose views differ from their own, not to judge others according to their own standards, and not to attempt to impose these standards on society. To regard a person who has a homosexual orientation with prejudice or disdain is entirely against the spirit of the Faith. And where occasion demands, it would be appropriate to speak out or act against unjust or oppressive measures directed towards homosexuals.

The Universal House of Justice. (2014) *Letter to Individual Believer*, May 9.

2.   According to the Bahá'í Teachings, marriage is a union between a man and a woman, and sexual relations are only permissible between a couple who are married to each other. This is set forth in the Writings of Bahá'u'lláh and in the authoritative statements of 'Abdu'l-Bahá and Shoghi Effendi and is not susceptible to change by the House of Justice. However, the Bahá'í community does not seek to impose its values on others and does not pass judgement on others on the basis of its own moral standards. Rather, Bahá'u'lláh enjoins the believers to manifest tolerance and respect towards all, and therefore, to regard those with a homosexual orientation with prejudice or disdain would be entirely against the spirit of the Faith.

The Universal House of Justice. (2009) *Letter to Individual Believer*, December 22

3.   The doors are open for all of humanity to enter the Cause of God, irrespective of their present circumstances; this invitation applies to homosexuals as well as any others who are engaged in practices contrary to the Bahá'í teachings.

The Universal House of Justice. (1995) *to a National Spiritual Assembly*, September 11

FOOD FOR THOUGHT:

- How do Bahá'ís view the expression of love between individuals of the same sex?
- What happens when someone who identifies themselves as homosexual wants to become a Bahá'í?

4. In a letter written on his behalf concerning the Bahá'í teachings on homosexuality, Shoghi Effendi explained that "the young believers in question must adhere to their Faith, and not withdraw from active service, because of the tests they experience. In one way or another, we are all tested; and this must strengthen us, not weaken us." All Bahá'ís struggle to meet the Bahá'í standard in different ways, and this effort is, except in limited circumstances, between the individual and God. The attitude an individual believer is to hold toward the imperfections of others is explicitly set forth. We are to be forbearing, concerned with our own shortcomings and not the shortcomings of others; we are to dwell only on good qualities and ignore the bad; and we are not to gossip, backbite, or "breathe … the sins of others". Yet, we are not to deny or contend with the authoritative texts, try to impose personal views on others, or insist that the community evolve in a manner that conforms to our personal desires. Thus, it is entirely against the spirit of the Bahá'í teachings to regard those who have a homosexual orientation with prejudice and disdain. At the same time, all Bahá'ís embrace the teachings of Bahá'u'lláh in their entirety and make every effort to uphold the standards set forth.

The Universal House of Justice. (2011) *Letter to Individual Believer*, July 21

FOOD FOR THOUGHT:

- What is Shoghi Effendi's guidance to young believers, according to this passage?

5. God judges each soul on its own merits. The Guardian cannot tell you what the attitude of God would be towards a person who lives a good life in most ways, but not in this way. All he can tell you is that it is forbidden by Bahá'u'lláh, and that one so afflicted should struggle and struggle again to overcome it. We must be hopeful of God's mercy but not impose upon it.

Shoghi Effendi. (1950) *Letter to Individual Believer*, March 26

6. The Bahá'í attitude towards the condition of homosexuality differs from its attitude towards those who engage in homosexual practices. The Guardian states that a Bahá'í who faces this challenge must strive daily to come closer to the Bahá'í standard and, in this process, should be treated with tolerance and receive help, advice, and sympathy. In one instance he encouraged the believers in question to adhere to their Faith and not to withdraw from active service because of the tests they experienced. In this connection, it may be helpful to consider that the challenge of striving to live a chaste and holy life is one that confronts every Bahá'í who is seeking to align his life with the principles of the Faith.

The Universal House of Justice. (2009) *Letter to Individual Believer*, December 22

7. Man's physical existence on this earth is a period during which the moral exercise of his free will is tried and tested in order to prepare his soul for the other worlds of God, and we must welcome affliction and tribulations as opportunities for improvement in our eternal selves. The House of Justice points out that homosexuals are not the only segment of human society labouring at this daily task — every human being is beset by such inner promptings as pride, greed, selfishness, lustful heterosexual or homosexual desires, to name a few which must be overcome, and overcome them we must if we are to fulfil the purpose of our human existence.

The Universal House of Justice. (1980) *Letter to Individual Believer*, July 16

FOOD FOR THOUGHT:

- Both lustful *heterosexual* and *homosexual* desires are considered to be inner promptings. What does it mean by "inner promptings"? List some examples. (You may use whiteboard)

8. The contemporary discussion surrounding homosexuality, which began in the West and is increasingly promoted in other parts of the world, generally takes the form of a false dichotomy, which compels one to choose between a position that is either affirming or rejecting. It is understandable that Bahá'ís would be sensitive to acts of prejudice or oppression in any form and to the needs of those who suffer as a result. But to align with either side in the public debate is to accept the premises on

which it is based. Moreover, this debate occurs within the context of a rising tide of materialism and consequent reorientation of society, over more than a century, which has among its outcomes a destructive emphasis on sexuality.

The Universal House of Justice. (2014) *Letter to Individual Believer*, May 9

9. Self-indulgence, in the guise of expressing one's true nature, becomes the norm, even the touchstone of healthy living. Consequently, sexuality has become a preoccupation, pervading commerce, media, the arts, and popular culture, influencing disciplines such as medicine, psychology, and education and reducing the human being to an object. It is no longer merely a part of life, but becomes the defining element of a person's identity. At its most extreme, the doctrine aggressively propagated in some societies is that it is abnormal for adolescents to restrain their sexual impulses, unreasonable for young adults to marry without first having had sexual relations, and impossible for a married couple to remain monogamous. The unbounded expression of sexuality in almost any form is thought to be natural and is accepted as a matter of course, the only limitation being to cause no harm to others, while any notion to the contrary is deemed narrow-minded or retrogressive. The question of same-sex marriage arises not simply as an appeal for fairness within a framework of existing values but as another step, presumed to be inevitable, in clearing away the vestiges of what is regarded to be a repressive traditional morality.

The Universal House of Justice. (2014) *Letter to Individual Believer*, May 9

FOOD FOR THOUGHT:

- Discuss examples where sexuality has become a preoccupation that has pervaded the following:
    - Commerce
    - Media
    - Social media
    - Arts
    - Popular culture
    - Medicine

    ❧ Psychology

    ❧ Education

❧ We are spiritual human beings that should be defined by our spiritual attributes. Why is it harmful to identify ourselves purely by our sexuality or in other words purely as a material/physical being?

❧ What elements should make up a person's true identity?

❧ Why is choosing a position of either affirmation or rejection of homosexuality a false dichotomy?

10. Although they affirm their conviction that Bahá'u'lláh's teachings reflect God's purpose for humankind in this Day, Bahá'ís do not seek to impose their values on others. They do not pass judgement on others on the basis of their own moral standards and can never presume to know the standing of any soul in the eyes of God. Rather, the friends are enjoined to show forth unconditional love, to engage in fellowship with all, and to be forbearing, concerned with their own shortcomings and not those of others. They are to have a sin-covering eye, focusing on good qualities and ignoring the bad, and they must eschew backbiting and gossip. As the Bahá'í community continues to grow and develop, increasing its involvement with the wider society, such characteristics will become more pronounced and a hallmark of Bahá'í culture.

The Universal House of Justice. (2013) *Letter to Individual Believer*, April 22

11. Bahá'ís must also be on their guard lest condemnatory attitudes stemming from the public debate take root in their communities. Backbiting and gossip, prejudice and estrangement, have no place. All recognize the need to transform themselves in accordance with Bahá'u'lláh's Teachings, all struggle in different ways to live a Bahá'í life, and there is no reason that the challenge of being attracted to persons of the same sex should be singled out and treated differently from other challenges. The Guardian made it clear that Bahá'ís with a homosexual orientation should not withdraw from the community and should receive its support and encouragement. The House of Justice sympathizes deeply with those individuals, and their families, who strive in this respect to understand and hold fast to the Teachings while buffeted by the controversy unfolding within their societies.

The Universal House of Justice. (2014) *Letter to Individual Believer*, May 9

- With reference to the quotes, how should one address the subject of homosexuality in the spirit of the Faith?
- Why is it important that one does not impose these standards on society?
- What harm is done when one judges others?

12. Across different cultures and within different societies there are, of course, many individuals and groups with diverse views or practices that, in one or more ways, are not in keeping with aspects of the Bahá'í Teachings. In this respect, the instance you cite is no different from many other situations — for example, that of a confirmed atheist or a devoted believer of another religion, a committed political activist, or an individual whose habits, manner of living, or moral convictions are at variance with the standards set forth by Bahá'u'lláh. In considering how to respond to such situations, it may be helpful to reflect upon fundamental principles and admonitions about teaching the Faith. The teacher should not contend with anyone, nor concentrate on proving to others that their beliefs or way of life are wrong. Rather, the goal of teaching is to assist the seeker to recognize the station of Bahá'u'lláh so that, out of love for His Beauty, he or she will accept whatever has been revealed by His Pen. Ultimately, however, there must be a hearing ear. As Bahá'u'lláh states:

> *Consort with all men, O people of Bahá, in a spirit of friendliness and fellowship. If ye be aware of a certain truth, if ye possess a jewel, of which others are deprived, share it with them in a language of utmost kindliness and goodwill. If it be accepted, if it fulfills its purpose, your object is attained. If anyone should refuse it, leave him unto himself, and beseech God to guide him. Beware lest ye deal unkindly with him.*

Thus, whether someone is interested in becoming a Bahá'í or not, Bahá'ís are encouraged to associate with all humanity in a manner governed by tolerance, unity, and love. Given the polemical nature of discussions concerning homosexuality in many societies, the friends should avoid being drawn into the debate, lest they be led to one or another extreme, either compromising Bahá'u'lláh's Teachings by weighing them according to contemporary social standards or allowing judgmental and prejudicial attitudes to creep into their community life.

The Universal House of Justice. (2014) *Letter to an individual believer,* July 7

Role play-

One person plays the role of a person who identifies themselves as a homosexual and the other; a Bahá'í who is their friend. The one who describes themselves as homosexual enquires from the Bahá'í youth about their personal thoughts and the Bahá'í views on homosexuality.

The Bahá'í youth should provide a response and dialogue that is compassionate, respectful, insightful and reflective of the learning in this section. Each pair will practice and then perform their role play for the group. After the presentations the group can consult on the approach taken in the role plays and if they feel it is effective and in line with the unifying spirit of the Faith.

WORKSHEET 4

(Homosexuality)

1. How do the Bahá'í Writings explain how we should view the expression of homosexuality?

2. According to the Bahá'í Writings, how should a person, who identifies themselves as homosexual be addressed or treated by other Bahá'ís?

3. Explain ways in which judgement and backbiting can lead to disunity.

SECTION 5

Chastity In All Religious Texts

1. Lax behaviour, broken observances and dubious chastity – these are of no great benefit.

    (Buddhist, Dhammapada – Sayings of the Buddha 1)

2. Therefore on account of (passages) of the revealed texts, and on account of the visible results, some declare these orders (of men keeping the vow of chastity to be) the most excellent.

    (The Dharma Sutras, Apastamba Prasna 2, Patala 9, Khanda 23, no.9)

3. Thus are praised those who keep the vow of chastity.

    (The Dharma Sutras, Apastamba Prasna 2, Patala 9, Khanda 23, no.6)

4. Allah's Apostle said, "Whoever can guarantee (the chastity of) what is between his two jaw-bones and what is between his two legs (i.e. his tongue and his private parts), I guarantee Paradise for him."

    (Hadith, Bukhari: Volume 8, Book 76, Number 481)

5. "Nor come near to adultery…for it is a shameful deed and an evil road (to other evils)."

    (Qur'an, 17:32)

6. "Indeed, the Muslim men and Muslim women, the believing men and believing women, the obedient men and obedient women, the truthful men and truthful women, the patient men and patient women, the humble men and humble women, the charitable men and charitable women, the fasting men and fasting women, the men who guard their private parts and the women who do so, and the men who remember Allah often and the women who do so – for them Allah has prepared forgiveness and a great reward."

    (Quran, 33:35)

7. Purity and stillness give the correct law to all under heaven.

    (Tao, Tao Te Ching)

8.   The spiritual man judgeth also by allowing of what is right, and disallowing what he finds amiss, in the works and lives of the faithful; their alms, as it were the earth bringing forth fruit, and of the living soul, living by the taming of the affections, in chastity, in fasting, in holy meditations; and of those things, which are perceived by the senses of the body.

Saint Augustine. (1921). Confessions of St Augustine. The Floating Press, p. 425.

9.   For this is the will of God, your sanctification: that you abstain from sexual immorality.

(*1 Thessalonians 4:3*, New International Version)

10.   But I say to you that everyone who looks at a woman with lustful intent has already committed adultery with her in his heart.

(*Matthew 5:35*, New International Version)

11.   This is the will of God, your holiness: that you refrain from immorality, that each of you knows how to acquire a wife for himself in holiness and honour, not in lustful passion as do the Gentiles who do not know God; not to take advantage of or exploit a brother in this matter, for the Lord is an avenger in all these things, as we told you before and solemnly affirmed. For God did not call us to impurity but to holiness.

(1 Thessalonians 4:3-7, New International Version)

12.   The Lord loves the pure of heart; the man of winning speech has the king for his friend.

(*Proverbs 22:11*, New International Version)

13.   Let marriage be honoured among all and the marriage bed be kept undefiled, for God will judge the immoral and adulterers.

(*Hebrew 13:4*, New International Version)

- Discuss some similarities between these religious scriptures on the topic of chastity.
- Discuss how the wisdom provided on chastity may differ due to the time and context in which they were revealed.

WORKSHEET 5

(Chastity in all religious texts)

What are some similarities and differences in the ways in which religions have explained the laws of chastity?

SECTION 6

Reflections

1. He feels that the youth, in particular, must constantly and determinedly strive to exemplify Bahá'í life. In the world around us we see moral decay, promiscuity, indecency, vulgarity, bad manners — the Bahá'í young people must be the opposite of these things, and, by their chastity, their uprightness, their decency, their consideration and good manners, attract others, old and young, to the Faith. The world is tired of words; it wants example, and it is up to the Bahá'í youth to furnish it.

    Shoghi Effendi. (1946) *Letter to Bahá'í Youth who attended the Green Acre Summer School*, September 19

2. A very great responsibility for the future peace and well-being of the world is borne by the youth of today. Let the Bahá'í youth by the power of the Cause they espouse be the shining example for their companions."

    The Universal House of Justice. (1965) *Letter to The National Spiritual Assembly of the United States*, April 15

FOOD FOR THOUGHT:

- Give concrete examples to illustrate the following:
    - Moral decay
    - Promiscuity
    - Indecency
    - Vulgarity
    - Bad manners
- Give concrete examples to illustrate the following:
    - Chastity
    - Uprightness
    - Decency
    - Consideration
    - Good manners

3. ...[T]here is nothing in the Bahá'í Writings which relates specifically to the so-called dating practices prevalent in some parts of the world, where two unmarried people

of the opposite sex participate together in a social activity. In general, Bahá'ís who are planning to involve themselves in this form of behavior should become well aware of the Bahá'í Teachings on chastity and, with these in mind, should scrupulously avoid any actions which would arouse passions which might well tempt them to violate these Teachings. In deciding which acts are permissible in the light of these considerations, the youth should use their own judgment, giving due consideration to the advice of their parents, taking account of the prevailing customs of the society in which they live, and prayerfully following the guidance of their conscience. It is the sacred duty of parents to instill in their children the exalted Bahá'í standard of moral conduct, and the importance of adherence to this standard cannot be over-emphasized as a basis for true happiness and for successful marriage.

The Universal House of Justice. (1992) *Letter to Individual Believer*, February 5

FOOD FOR THOUGHT:

- Having learned about the concept of the lower and higher nature, how can one decide which of one's actions are permissible?

4. Consultation bestoweth greater awareness and transmuteth conjecture into certitude. It is a shining light which, in a dark world, leadeth the way and guideth. For everything there is and will continue to be a station of perfection and maturity. The maturity of the gift of understanding is made manifest through consultation.

Bahá'u'lláh (1985), *Tablet cited in The Promise of World Peace, Haifa: The Universal House of Justice*, p.15.

FOOD FOR THOUGHT:

- Do youth readily consult with their parents about chastity and its broader implications? Why or why not?
- What are some benefits of consulting with parents/guardians on the broader implications of chastity that affect the lives of youth?

5. Although a Bahá'í may, if he chooses, seek his parents' advice on the choice of a partner, and although Bahá'í parents may give such advice if asked, it is clear from the Teachings that parents do not have the right to interfere in their children's actual choice of a prospective partner until approached for their consent to marry.

The Universal House of Justice. (1994) *Letter to Individual Believer*, August 28

6. The first condition is absolute love and harmony amongst the members of the assembly. They must be wholly free from estrangement and must manifest in themselves the Unity of God, for they are the waves of one sea, the drops of one river, the stars of one heaven, the rays of one sun, the trees of one orchard, the flowers of one garden. Should harmony of thought and absolute unity be nonexistent, that gathering shall be dispersed and that assembly be brought to naught. The second condition is that the members of the assembly should unitedly elect a chairman and lay down guide-lines and by-laws for their meetings and discussions. The chairman should have charge of such rules and regulations and protect and enforce them; the other members should be submissive, and refrain from conversing on superfluous and extraneous matters. They must, when coming together, turn their faces to the Kingdom on high and ask aid from the Realm of Glory. They must then proceed with the utmost devotion, courtesy, dignity, care and moderation to express their views. They must in every matter search out the truth and not insist upon their own opinion, for stubbornness and persistence in one's views will lead ultimately to discord and wrangling and the truth will remain hidden. The honoured members must with all freedom express their own thoughts, and it is in no wise permissible for one to belittle the thought of another…

'Abdu'l-Bahá 1982, *Selections from the Writings of 'Abdu'l-Bahá, Bahá'í World Centre*, Haifa, p.88-89.

FOOD FOR THOUGHT:

- Using the guidance read about consultation for assemblies, what are some of the spiritual qualities needed for a healthy consultation? Give concrete examples where possible.

7. Throughout the world, in diverse cultures, Bahá'ís encounter values and practices that stand in sharp contrast to the teachings of the Faith. Some are embedded in social structures, for instance, racial prejudice and gender discrimination, economic exploitation and political corruption. Others pertain to personal conduct, especially with respect to the use of alcohol and drugs, to sexual behaviour, and to self-indulgence in general. If Bahá'ís simply surrender to the mores of society, how will conditions change? How will the people of the world distinguish today's moribund order from the civilization to which Bahá'u'lláh is summoning humanity? "Humanity", the Ridván 2012 message of the House of Justice explained, "is weary for want of a pattern of life to which to aspire." "A single soul can uphold a standard far above the low threshold by which the world measures itself," the message noted. Young Bahá'ís especially need to take care, lest they imagine they can live according to the norms of contemporary society while adhering to Bahá'í ideals at some minimum level to assuage their conscience or to satisfy the community, for they will soon find themselves consumed in a struggle to obey even the most basic of the Faith's moral teachings and powerless to take up the challenges of their generation. "Wings that are besmirched with mire can never soar," Bahá'u'lláh warns. The inner joy that every individual seeks, unlike a passing emotion, is not contingent on outside influences; it is a condition, born of certitude and conscious knowledge, fostered by a pure heart, which is able to distinguish between that which has permanence and that which is superficial.

The Universal House of Justice. (2013) *Letter to Individual Believer*, April 19

FOOD FOR THOUGHT:

- What are some dangers of living according to the norms and standards of contemporary society and not the standards outlined in the Bahá'í writings?

8. The duty to obey the laws brought by Bahá'u'lláh for a new age, then, rests primarily on the individual believer. It lies at the heart of the relationship of the lover and the Beloved; "Observe My commandments, for the love of My beauty," is Bahá'u'lláh's exhortation. Yet what is expected in this connection is effort sustained by earnest desire, not instantaneous perfection. The qualities and habits of thought and action that characterize Bahá'í life are developed through daily exertion. "Bring thyself to

account each day", writes Bahá'u'lláh. "Let each morn be better than its eve", He advises, "and each morrow richer than its yesterday." The friends should not lose heart in their personal struggles to attain to the Divine standard, nor be seduced by the argument that, since mistakes will inevitably be made and perfection is impossible, it is futile to exert an effort. They are to steer clear of the pitfalls of hypocrisy, on the one hand — that is, saying one thing yet doing another — and heedlessness, on the other — that is, disregard for the laws, ignoring or explaining away the need to follow them. So too is paralysis engendered by guilt to be avoided; indeed, preoccupation with a particular moral failing can, at times, make it more challenging for it to be overcome.

The Universal House of Justice. (2013) *Letter to Individual Believer*, April 19

FOOD FOR THOUGHT:

- As we strive daily to align our actions with the standard set in the Bahá'í Faith, what does the Universal House of Justice direct us to do in the context of the quote above?
- How can we avoid being paralyzed by guilt?
- How can a preoccupation with a moral failing make it more challenging for it to be overcome?

9. The more difficulties one sees in the world the more perfect one becomes. The more you plough and dig the ground the more fertile it becomes. The more you cut the branches of a tree the higher and stronger it grows. The more you put the gold in the fire the purer it becomes. The more you sharpen the steel by grinding the better it cuts. Therefore, the more sorrows one sees the more perfect one becomes. That is why, in all times, the Prophets of God have had tribulations and difficulties to withstand. The more often the captain of a ship is in the tempest and difficult sailing the greater his knowledge becomes. Therefore I am happy that you have had great tribulations and difficulties. For this I am very happy — that you have had many sorrows. Strange it is that I love you and still I am happy that you have sorrows.

'Abdu'l-Bahá, 1923, *Star of the West*, vol. 14, no. 2, p. 41.

- In what ways can one view difficulties as blessings?
- Will following the laws of God and chastity be easy? Why or why not?
- What are some tests that we may face when trying to follow the laws?
- Knowing that following the laws may involve a series of victories and of shortcomings, what does practicing chastity with a posture of learning look like?

WORKSHEET 6

(Reflections)

1. What insights have you gained about the role of youth today?

2. Why shouldn't we judge how others choose to live their life?

3. In what ways can it be helpful to discuss issues related to chastity with our parents, guardians or institution members? Name some examples where a discussion may be beneficial to you and those around you.

4. Make a list of spiritual insights you have gained from deepening on *Purify My Heart*, which you will share and practice with your communities:

1)

2)

3)

4)

5)

APPENDIX

A selection of relevant resources:

(1976). *A Compilation on Bahá'í Education.* Haifa: Bahá'í World Centre.

Bahá'u'lláh, Abdu'l-Bahá, Shoghi Effendi and Universal House of Justice (1991). *A Compilation of Compilations: A Chaste and Holy Life*, Mona Vale: Bahai Publications Australia.

Baha'i Publishing (2009). *Marriage: A Fortress for Well-Being.* Wilmette: Baha'i Publishing Trust.

Shoghi Effendi (1990). *The Advent of Divine Justice.* Wilmette: Bahá'í Publishing Trust.

Universal House of Justice. (2013) *Letter to a group of individuals on behalf of the Universal House of Justice*, April 19

Universal House of Justice. (2014) *Letter to an individual believer*, May 9

Universal House of Justice. (2013) *Letter to a National Spiritual Assembly*, April 23